THE ADVENTURER'S GUIDE TO AUDIOBOOKS

THE ADVENTURER'S GUIDE TO AUDIOBOOKS

A SELF-PUBLISHING WALKTHROUGH

DANIEL RYDER
AND
HEATHER RYDER

Inkling Books

Cover art by Almir Gusić
@almirgusic on Instagram

Inkling Books, LLC
Raleigh, North Carolina
www.inklingbookspublishing.com

Ordering Information:
For details, contact daniel@inklingbookspublishing.com.

Print ISBN: 979-8-9916764-4-1
eBook ISBN: 979-8-9916764-5-8
Audiobook ISBN: 979-8-9916764-6-5
First Edition

Acknowledgments

Thank you to all the folks who were willing to let us talk their ears off as we formulated this book. Special thanks for the wonderful insights and valuable corrections we received from our alpha and beta readers: Adam, my Brooke, your Brooke (you know who is who), Chase, Ian, Jaye, Jennifer, Kevin, Louise, Rebecca, Ricky, Sareek, and Will.

Also, a shout-out to our fantastic contributing artists: Almir Gusić (illustrator of the front cover) and Thomas Moonjeli (our photographer).

DISCLAIMER

This book is an unofficial, nerdy, and highly affectionate guide to the strange and wonderful world of publishing. It contains parody characters and references to familiar fantasy archetypes for the sake of humor, education, and satire.

In particular, the character Grandalf the Prismatic is a wholly original creation. While he may remind you of other famous wizards with big hats and firm opinions, he is intended as a loving parody and educational mascot—here to demystify publishing, not to cast copyrighted spells. This work is not affiliated with, endorsed by, or associated with the Tolkien Estate, Middle-earth Enterprises, or any related properties.

All characters in this book are fictitious, pixelated, or chaotic goblins. Any resemblance to real publishing professionals, living or dead, is probably a coincidence . . . but also kind of flattering.

LEGEND

How to Use This Book

To Our Readers:

We think that authors should be able to bring their stories into the world without being stopped by a lack of knowledge or resources. And to that end, we wanted to put together this little guide that speaks to our people: the nerds, gamers, anime lovers, and convention chasers.

There are a few concessions we ask you to give us as you start this book. The first is to understand that even though we know what we're talking about, we always have room to err (yes, despite her dwarf-like penchant for hammers, Heather is still human). We can only share from the knowledge we have acquired in our life; while that is limited in scope, it is still extensive compared to many.

Daniel has recorded quite a few audiobooks of varying length (30 at the time of this publication), and yet they are not an academically trained audio engineer. They are, instead, a trained actor and a chemist (in that order).

Heather, who stepped onto the yellow-book road at a young age, graduated with a degree in English Lit and Creative Writing and has been in the editing world for more than ten years, spanning work for big companies (ever heard of Wiley?) and for individual, self-published authors.

And yet, with all our shared experience and passion in the field, we still get our fair share of imposter syndrome. We're going to share what has worked for us and, hopefully, light a torch to brighten what is otherwise an incredibly obscure path. There are traps filled with grammar rules, noise floors, fonts, DAWs, mirrored margins . . . and watch out for those AI mimics! We've had our share of mistakes, and will continue to have more, but the point is that we learn from them. From this book, please take what is useful, laugh at what's funny, and throw the rest in your mental recycle bin.

Additionally, we want this book to talk to you as if you are in the room. That is why we wrote it in second person and structured it as a choose your own adventure—the end of each chapter will provide you with an opportunity to decide which section you would like to jump to next. This was done partially for novelty and partially because Daniel's older brother gifted them a choose-your-own-adventure series when they were very young, and that series lives in Daniel's head rent free.

Our hope is that we wrote this book in a way that, regardless of how you read it—front-to-back, jumping around, or back-to-front (I mean, if you *really* want to . . .)—the sections will read well and easily. The chapter titles should give you an idea of what each section is going to be focusing on, so if you wish to jump straight to a specific topic, the legend (table of contents) in the beginning should be able to point you to the right page.

Oh, and a final note about why we even do this: we're nerds. We love books and the authors who write them. It takes a special kind of person to look at the world and decide that they want to add a piece of magic that explores the depths of what it is to be human. That magic lets us wrestle with the truths of humanity by putting us in alien worlds, isolating valuable contexts of our shared reality.

There are probably hundreds if not thousands of books that talk about the path to publishing in dry, highbrow terms and rules, so we wanted to share our take with a fun, theatrical bit of flimflam.

Happy reading (and chuckling, hopefully),

Daniel and Heather

"THE END"

You emerge from a deep brain fog, fingers stiff and aching from overuse. You reach for your coffee mug, hoping for a few more drops of the life-giving liquid. Empty. You must have drunk it all sometime between the final showdown and the hero's resounding triumph. You stare down at the light-brown ring that's stained the wood of your desk. You really need to get one of the coasters from . . . goddamn, where *do* you keep those anyway? Maybe you should just accept the stains and lean into it.

You look back up at the screen to see your final words floating next to the flashing cursor. Was it really finished? All these months of work, years of thought, not to mention constant drain on your passive mental processing . . . Just keeping track of this world's magic system has left you too distracted to track some of your friends' conversations in the real, non-magical world. Or maybe they're just boring? No, that couldn't be it.

The cursor continues to flash, tempting you to write another word. Another sentence. The story couldn't possibly be done. Well, a writer's work is never done—creativity has no end. But what the hell is next?

Suddenly, an image appears on the screen in front of you! It looks like a tiny wizard, almost chibi-like, and yet he seems familiar. He somehow reminds you of a cross between the Fourth Doctor and . . . Mithrandir? The pixelated wizard tips his pointed hat at you and speaks in an accented voice that is at once both kindly and firm, though a bit high-pitched.

"It may be that you wish the gift of story writing had not been foisted upon you. So do I, and so do all who have lived to see such stories wrought on the pages of their making. But that is not for you to decide. All you can do is decide what to write with the gift that was given to you."

Your brain jumps back to the notification you received earlier about your antivirus software being out of date. But you could have sworn you hadn't gone to any skeevy websites. So what the hell was this little guy? And was he . . . British? Your browser must really be letting its security go to shit.

As if reading your mind, the tiny wizard shouts out in a squeaky voice, "DO NOT TAKE ME FOR SOME CORRUPTER WITH CHEAP TRICKS! I am not an infection upon your system, nor do I wish to mine your data. I am trying to help you. *Now*, will you listen?"

Certainly a weird way to try and convince someone that you're not a virus. A novel approach at least? Feeling silly, you nod slowly to the tiny wizard.

"Good. Now, let's get introductions out of the way. I am Grandalf the Prismatic." As he announces himself, he gives a grand twirl of his digital cloak, making it flash with a repeating waterfall of bright colors. You can't help but smirk at the early 2000s animation.

"Yes, yes, very funny," he grumbles, "but we don't have time for that now! Thankfully, it seems you understand that I am not here to harm. It appears that you have gotten to the end of your story and are now ready to take the next steps in the grand adventure that is sharing your book with the world. You do not have the look of one who knows what comes next. Would you like me to help—"

Before he can finish, however, another digital figure pops up beside him. They bop Grandalf's staff, making him drop a few pixels below the screen.

This figure looks like they came straight out of a D&D adventure path: a short goblinoid with pointed ears, green skin, and an overly wide mouth that might be full of sharp teeth (the pixels aren't quite detailed enough for you to be certain).

Either way, they give you a big, toothy grin and say, "Buttercup the Bard, at your service! It is always an honor to go on an adventure with a noble story writer!"

You notice they are wearing a stylish red-leather cloak, have a lute strapped to their side, and are sporting a bright yellow flower in their front breast pocket.

Hesitantly, you ask, "Aren't you normally a human? Also, I thought in the game you were named Dandeli–"

"Shhhh! No, it's Buttercup! For copyright reasons, I cannot stress enough that I am *Buh-ter-cup*. Got it?" the goblin says shrilly, baring their teeth at you.

Yup, definitely sharp, pointy teeth. You nod.

"Ok, good. Now, Grandalf here skipped my cue, so let me explain. The old man may be able to guide you through all the basics of printing your story, but as someone who actually sells their talents to passing strangers, *I* can tell you all the valuable information of how to con– I mean, *convince* folks to pay you money for your story!"

As you process this, a third figure strides on to your screen, dressed to the nines and looking like he's about to tell you to "go long on Apple" or "short on crypto." He's got a classy suit, his hair is styled, and he somehow walks across your screen exuding bytes of confidence.

"Now, now, Buttercup, don't go making them think *you* handle the money. You know that's my area of expertise!" he says, crossing his arms.

A little animated cloud pops out of Buttercup's mouth as they huff and the businessman nods in acceptance before turning to you. "Excellent. Now, where were we? That's right, this new book of yours. It's a big step investing in yourself. You should be proud of the work you've done. By the way, the name's Richard. It is an absolute pleasure to meet you. Congratulations on reaching 'The End.'"

You take a moment to consider—you shouldn't shake his hand with the cursor, should you? I mean, it is the old 90s one that's shaped like a hand. No. No, that would be ridiculous. Clearly the answer is to shut down the computer and take it to an exorcist.

"Just a moment!" Grandalf pipes up with almost telepathic timing. "Do not waste this opportunity. We three are here to show you the way, and all we ask is that you tell us what you wish to know and heed our wisdom! So, where shall we start?"

As he asks this, a little dialogue box with three options pops up:

"I want to make my book ready to share, but I do not know the way."

<Turn to page 9>

"I have friends who've critiqued my book, and I'm a careful writer. Why do people say I need an editor?"

<Turn to page 15>

"I'm ready to record my book for readers who like to listen! How do I set my space up for recording?"

<Turn to page 48>

I DO NOT KNOW THE WAY

Grandalf looks kindly at you. Well, the pixels approximate a kindly expression. Buttercup and Richard both hop up and disappear with a click.

"A humble choice. The first thing we must talk about is beta reading then." He pauses. "Oh, you say bay-ta here, don't you? Well, do you know what a beta reader is?"

You find yourself shaking your head. The term sounds familiar, and you have a good guess what they might be, but you don't remember specific details.

"A beta reader allows you to get a sense of how your audience might respond to your story. It's a lot like beta testing in game development–you let people explore your partially tested project, gather all their feedback, and then use those to improve your book. That's also usually when an editor should jump in to help. Sometimes the feedback is as simple as needing to change a word or clarify some local lingo. For example, I might write a story about my characters often enjoying elevenses, but readers from your region would likely be clueless to the wonderful bliss that is elevenses.

"Other times, you might receive some feedback that results in major rewrites or restructuring of the book. Beta readers are especially good at giving you a fresh perspective on characters and settings that you don't personally have much knowledge in. Want your characters to be streetwise in Chicago? Get a beta reader who grew up in Chicago.

"Now here, take a look at this." Grandalf waves his staff over his head, and your cursor starts to move with it. Your manuscript gets minimized and with a double click, your web browser opens. The letters "B E T A [space] R E A–" begin getting typed out at a painstaking pace until a familiar, sharp voice pipes up.

"I told you, old man, you gotta use both hands. All the fingers! Now stop that." Buttercup pops up again and pushes Grandalf's staff back to the ground.

"Look, Grandalf is right that you need to make sure to pick beta readers who will give you valuable information. What he failed to mention, though, is how you should deal with feedback you receive. See, these readers don't know your story, and they don't have your voice. Only you have that. *But*, before you go dismissing any critiques that you think are shi–" Grandalf gives Buttercup a light thwack on the head.

They huff. "Shipoopy . . . grouchy old cuss. Anyway, they're usually on to something. We like to say that readers have good instincts for where something's off, *but* how to solve that problem is your job—and if you've found an editor who understands your voice, theirs too!

"I know when I had beta readers look over my first book, I had a lot of readers tell me they couldn't stand the main character. While my first instinct was to tell them to get f— ahem, *stuffed,* after scanning through their comments, I noticed that the readers' complaints were mostly in the beginning, and toward the end they were actually complimenting my MC. I realized that I just needed to move some background and fun bits from the end of the story to the beginning, and *voila*! A likable character from the start."

Grandalf, who up till now has been tapping his foot impatiently, now has angry little squiggles hovering above his head.

Buttercup coughs lightly. "Uhh. Right, hurrying along. Key thing, have some combination of double-spaced, spiral-bound document you printed at Kinkos and a digital document that readers can comment on. Friends are a great place to start, and once you've gone through all of them, look online. There are plenty of forums, plus marketplaces like Fiverr and Upwork, which can be pretty affordable."

Grandalf gives a sparkly flip of his cloak and snaps, "Are you quite finished?"

"Eeek, sorry Grandalf." With a strum of their lute, Buttercup disappears.

"*Thank* you. Now, it seems we've gotten through the meat of what makes a beta reader useful, so it's about time we get on to the next section. We can talk about editors, or if you already have an editor lined up that you love, we could instead jump ahead to what you need to get your book ready for print or audio."

Grandalf gives you what seems to be an uncharacteristically mischievous look and starts to fade away by degrees, his voice echoing, "The choice is up to yoooooou."

Another dialogue box appears with three choices:

"I'm an incredibly careful writer, so do I really need an editor?"

<Turn to page 15>

"I've already got an editor on speed dial. How do I go about getting this thing formatted?"

<Turn to page 25>

"I want my book prepped for readers who like to listen! What tech do I need?"

<Turn to page 54>

THERE'S NO NEED FOR AN EDITOR, RIGHT?

Buttercup and Richard are nowhere to be seen. Before you have a chance to contemplate where they may have gone to, the tiny wizard moves to command the center of the screen and gives you a long, contemplative look.

"I understand your hesitation, but it all comes down to the thing that helped you create your story in the first place." He gestures toward you through the glass of the screen and says, "Your mind is so powerful that it can hold multiple stories or even multiple timelines for the same story at the same time. But that also means when you read through your work, your mind can auto-correct things in ways that cause you to miss things. Often only small things, but sometimes rather large ones. That's why getting a fresh set of eyes to do a detailed read of your story is absolutely essential.

"On top of which, there's the creative process to consider. We find that skilled storytellers like yourself do their best work when they focus all their energy on painting a work of art that their readers can get lost in, then entrust that to an editor to look over and empower. If you spend all your time obsessing over every word, you'll find that hinders your ability to actually write the story."

You frown, remembering the number of times you were locked between two equally excellent but meaningless distinctions. And then there was that article your writer friend sent you about the newspaper that accidentally put "pubic" instead of "public" in their headline . . .

Grandalf nods at you knowingly and continues. "At this stage, it's most important to decide what kind of editing you need. Depending on how many drafts you've gone through, what type of writing style you have, and what kind of feedback you get from your beta readers, you'll need to choose between three levels of editing: developmental, copyediting, or proofreading." As he speaks, he waves his staff around wildly, and each word appears on your screen in a Paint pencil format, his scribbly handwriting only adding to the pixelated confusion.

"Ideally, if your budget allows, you can often find an editor that will help you with all three of these—a package service that gets your book from its current state to ready-to-print."

He points at "developmental" and says, "This kind of editing addresses things like flow, plot development, character motivations, and narrative consistency. If you decided to write some of your chapters in first person and some in third, for example, an editor can help you decide whether that fits the style you're going for.

"Also, if you haven't already, putting your characters into some sort of reference sheet can help you and your editor catalog each character, noting their names, relations, significance, et cetera."

You sigh. That sounds like a lot of work.

Buttercup's sharp voice comes out of nowhere, saying, "Oooor you could just let all your readers bitch on Goodreads about how Saveen's name changed to 'Sabine' halfway through Chapter 7, and also, 'why on earth was she holding that knife after she had given it to her brother when she freed him from that prison?' Ask me how I know."

Grandalf frowns at the swear word, but he nods in agreement. "They're not wrong. You owe it to your dedicated readers to give them a good, clean story without inconsistencies. I can't tell you how many times small continuity errors pop up between edits, purely because you were focusing on some other element or detail.

"Once the big-picture details are settled, you want a copyeditor, also called a line editor." A 90s-era sparkle flashes next to Grandalf's eye while a banner animation tells you he's getting really pumped up. "*This* is where editors really shine. While other people decided they wanted 'a life,' editors learned how to go over grammar and syntax with the precision of an elven ranger piercing an orcish eye from across a field."

As Grandalf says this, Richard confidently side-steps onto the screen. "Careful, Grandalf, you don't wanna be rude to our dear writer! It almost sounds like you're telling them that their work is subpar."

The wizard looks back at him, aghast. "Not at all! I was simply saying that all writing needs editing, no matter the skill level of the writer."

Richard turns to look at you and says, "Editors, am I right?" He then turns back to Grandalf. "Grandy, you haven't explained the *relationship* between an editor and a writer. You've only mentioned all the ways they could have made mistakes."

Tear animations flash over Grandalf's head. "Richard, you make an excellent point. One which I regret I did not notice on my own. Thank you."

Richard turns and gives you a wink, saying, "You're welcome," and then saunters back off screen.

Grandalf takes a deep breath then turns back to look at you. "What I should have explained right out of the gate is that it's most important to find an editor who *understands* you and your writing. They need to connect with it, feel the beats of your story, and know how to retain your voice. The point isn't for them to try and make it their own work–it's for them to make your words *sing*.

"In addition to that, they should be able to give you feedback that is both constructive and kind. Being a self-proclaimed 'grammar nazi,' as I've heard the children saying, is *not* a guarantee of a good editor. You should be looking for an editor who has worked with books in a similar genre or style to yours."

You hear Richard shout from offscreen, "And just how should they go about finding this experienced editor?"

Buttercup's voice pipes up, "Yeah, someone who doesn't think their writing is crap!"

Grandalf stomps his foot and shouts grumpily, "How can one be expected to explain anything with all these interruptions? For goodness sake, I never even got to explain what proofreading is!"

Silence answers him. "Ahem, thank you." He points his staff up to the third word scrawled on the screen. "Let me explain proofreading, and then you can talk to Richard about finding an editor.

"Proofreading is similar to copyediting in that the editor will be looking for errors at a word-by-word level, but this specifically happens at the very final stage when the book is about to be sent off to the printer. Proofreaders look at the final manuscript to catch any remaining typos, misnumbered pages, mis-styled chapter headings, and awkward line breaks. Are you keeping up?"

You nod silently. After his last outburst, it might be best not to interrupt him.

"Good. Now, finding an editor. Richard?"

Richard saunters back onto the screen. "You got it, Grandy. Now, you can always ask a friend or colleague to go over your work on the cheap, but assuming it's not their main job, you will often find this is going to be the slowest option. Budget-friendly options with a bit faster pacing are going to be general platforms like Fiverr or Upwork, but it can be hard to vet the work they've done. Plus, there's those pesky fees.

"Dedicated editor platforms, such as Reedsy and the ACES Editors for Hire Directory, represent the next big step in terms of quality, but at a higher price. In this category, the most price efficient option is generally to hire an editor directly who has proof of their experience. There won't be any upcharge from a third-party platform, and these editors make their living off their work, so they'll be accountable." Richard finishes with a little bow, then disappears with a pop.

Grandalf begins pacing across the screen, ticking off fingers as he mutters, "Why use an editor . . . Types of editing . . . What to look for . . . How to find one . . ." He stops walking and turns to look at you, beaming. "I believe we have finally reached the end. Do you have any questions?"

Just as you open your mouth to speak, he jumps a little and cries, "Ah, of course! How does one know when their editor is a good fit? Always ask for a sample edit of a few pages, either of your own work or from something else they did in the past. This is often enough to determine whether you are . . . simpatico, if you will.

"Now, at the risk of repeating oneself, I believe that is everything. What would you like to explore for our next adventure?" He waves his staff and the onscreen words are wiped off as a new dialogue box pops up:

"Once I finish the editing, how do I go about getting it formatted?"

<Turn to page 25>

"I know the ins and outs of book formatting, but what about illustrating a book cover?"

<Turn to page 31>

"I'm ready to record my book! What tech do I need?"

<Turn to page 54>

How do I go about getting my book formatted?

You look away from the screen for a moment, wondering if you might need a fresh cup of coffee to focus up. Mouse-clicking noises snap your attention back to the screen, where you see Grandalf's avatar clapping his tiny hands.

He says, "Traditional publishing paths generally deal with book formatting so that you don't have to, but if you want to publish your book yourself, distributors will require you to format it properly.

"The burden of book formatting and printing—the typographic basilisk, if you will—is that once you know it, you will never be able to open a book and read it in the same way. The formatting process covers many details—book size, margins, gutters, chapter heading stylization, illustrations, font choices, and, of course, avoiding widows, orphans, and runts."

You raise your eyebrow at the last one.

Grandalf smiles back knowingly. "I thought you might be curious at that. In brief, solitary lines of text or individual words that hang awkwardly at the top or bottom of a page. If your curiosity leads you further, I suggest consulting the mirror of Googladriel."

"Grandalf, tell them about the magic of formatting! I always love how it all comes together," crows Buttercup from offscreen.

Grandalf continues, smiling, "When formatting is done well, it is not noticeable to the reader. It allows your work to speak for itself without distraction . . ." He begins pacing, then says grandly, "You want your readers to believe in the book before they even start it. Warriors do not come to

Elven smiths on reputation alone, you know. The shape and form of the work sells itself.

"How the words flow across the page is an essential piece of your printed tale, but illustration is also part of formatting, and that bit is a pretty picture."

He stops to laugh at his own joke before continuing, "Illustration is a great way to add more elements that build out your world. You can include symbols and letters unique to your realm, build sketches or maps that show the reader how your character got there and back again . . ." Grandalf stops to contemplate you more soberly, and you realize he is trying to discern if he might have given you more than you bargained for.

"Not to worry!" Grandalf says, more to himself than to you. "Many online distributors help outline all the details and requirements for you, so you are not left wandering about aimlessly. However, you still need a technological way to put all these details together, and this is often a choice between knowledge, money, and time. Richard?"

Richard ambles onto screen beside the tiny wizard and begins to list off the options as they simultaneously appear onscreen.

"Option 1: Do all the formatting yourself. The standard programs are things like Adobe InDesign, Atticus, and Scrivener. Microsoft Word can work but it's fairly limited. Doing it yourself gives you full creative control, but also means that you will be responsible for knowing and meeting all the distributors' requirements.

"Option 2: Ask your editor if they include formatting in their services. They might be willing to negotiate a package deal, which can be an excellent way to save money if you already have an editor you know and love. If your book is complicated to format, your editor should be able to tell you honestly what they can and can't do.

"Option 3: Hire out. This is another great place to work with a freelancer, such as those on Fiverr and Upwork, or find a professional who would be willing to work with you. This is often the most expensive option, but it lets you meet a much higher professional standard since you're usually going to be working with specialists.

"Option 1 saves you money, but will require time and knowledge, whereas options 2 and 3 cost money, but will save you the time and need for knowledge."

Richard turns back to Grandalf, nods, and strides confidently off screen. Grandalf, who has been watching Richard the whole time with a bemused expression, turns to you and asks, "Now, what would you like to learn about next?"

"How do I find an illustrator for my cover?"

<Turn to page 31>

"I've got the book cover . . . covered, but what the hell is an ISBN?"

<Turn to page 38>

"I've got all the main pieces of the book covered! What tech do I need for recording?"

<Turn to page 54>

How Do I Find an Illustrator?

Grandalf chuckles, then steps aside with an elegant twirl, and Richard walks on screen. He clasps his hands together and says cheerily, "Allow me to guide you in this! Finding an illustrator can be hard. Part of the problem is that art is subjective, so one person's magnum opus might be another person's marketing nightmare. It's incredibly valuable to do some market research before you choose an artist, and that's where *I* excel."

You look over at Grandalf, who has conjured a chair out of nowhere and is casually flipping through a book. He looks up at you to say simply, "It is best to let each share their own skills and talents."

Richard gives him a small nod and then turns back to look at you. "Take a moment to define what makes your book unique. What kind of story is it telling? And what are some other stories that you think are similar to yours?

"It's important to note here that you're not trying to make your book blend in with all the others. You're trying to narrow things down in order to isolate the big, high-performing books in your category, and *then* figure out what makes them stand out."

With a sudden flash of movement, Grandalf leaps out of his chair and waves his tome high in the air as he shouts, "A POOR BOOK COVER CANNOT PASS!"

There is an awkward silence as Richard gives him a long, hard stare, and Grandalf slowly sits back down, muttering to himself.

"Righto . . . You should be looking for images and designs that make you stop walking in a bookstore or stop you from scrolling further online. When you find works like that, take a photo, save the image, or write down what it was that made you stop and stare. Also, *please* do yourself a favor and figure out who the hell the artist was and write that down too. You'll want it for reference if you decide to hire that artist or if you want to show their work to someone else as an example."

Grandalf pipes up with a glint in his eye, "Richard, it's almost like you're saying you should judge a book by its cover."

"You absolutely *should* judge a book by its cover," Richard shoots back. "Maybe that didn't matter back when *you* were handwriting books on vellum, but in a *modern* world where there are 11,000 books being published every day, you need a way to stand out. If nobody notices your book enough to want to pick it up, it doesn't matter how well written it is. It could be the best book in existence, and it wouldn't matter a bit.

"Now, once you know your best-fitting genre, put it into the Amazon search bar and see what comes up in the top 10. Consider the cover images, colors, drawing styles, internal illustrations, and any other elements that make them stand out. Compare the notes you took on your preferences and the results you got from your search, then start incorporating those into something that represents your story.

"Does your main character have a unique weapon? Is there a distinct visual element to the magic in your world? Maybe there's something special about the city where the story takes place. How can you get that on the cover in a way that entices a reader to pick it up?

"Then, when you have all that in your head, you can either start sketching, find an online platform that has premade covers, or start looking for illustrators to hire.

"If you're doing this on your own, you could use some low budget options like Canva or PowerPoint, but the ideal programs are Adobe Illustrator or Photoshop.

"If you want to go the premade route, it is usually reasonably priced, but by the nature of the platforms, the cover designs will be more generic. The third option will almost certainly be the most costly, depending on who you hire, but it will result in the most thoughtful and high-quality cover or illustration."

Richard stops to take a long breath and looks over at Grandalf, who is still humming to himself as he thumbs through his book. Then he turns back to look at you.

"So, your options: do it yourself, pay for a template, or pay for a professional. Things to remember are that the art should be eye-catching but within the style of the appropriate genre, and at the end of the day your cover is marketing, pure and simple . . .

"OH! One last thing–if you do hire someone, make sure to ask if they will give you ongoing support, in case there's something wrong with the dimensions or specs or anything else. Better yet, if you can also get the original design files along with the image files, then you can save those files to be edited in the future by anyone else, if you need."

Grandalf stands up, his chair disappearing with a click. He starts to walk away, nose still buried in his book, and he mumbles distractedly, "Yes, yes, well done, Richard . . ."

Richard pipes up, "We can go over ISBNs, how to submit your final, print-ready book, or we can skip right along to the audio!"

"What the hell is an ISBN?"

<Turn to page 38>

"Show me how to submit my book for printing!"

<Turn to page 43>

"Let's talk audio. How do I get my space set up?"

<Turn to page 48>

What the Hell is an ISBN?

Grandalf looks profoundly disappointed by the question and walks fully off screen, mumbling something about "fool of a book . . ." As he leaves, Richard drifts over, giving you a shrug as he glances back at the wizard.

Spreading his arms out, Richard collects himself and says grandly, "International Standard Book Number! That's what an ISBN is, and it is needed for every book printed, every new edition, and every new format. So you'll need one for every book you write, every new edition you print, and every format you decide to produce—paperback, hardback, *and* audiobook.

Richard begins, "At some point a while ago, some genius—"

You hear Buttercup offscreen give a hacking cough that sounds suspiciously like "rich schmuck."

" . . . decided that books should be numbered in an internationally standardized organizational system, and he managed to convince publishers around the world that was a good idea. The number links the book to the country, region, and language of the book.

"Now, thanks to him, you'll need to buy some of these numbers in order to sell your book. In the US, you'll need to buy those numbers off a company named Bowker, the designated ISBN agency for the States. There are some printing agencies that will offer a free ISBN for you, like KDP and IngramSpark, but they'll restrict you selling on other platforms. Similarly, if you go through traditional publishing, the publisher will provide the ISBN because they technically own the book.

"I wanna note here that ISBNs are technically not required for eBooks. However, distributors like bookshops, libraries, and the like expect—and usually require—them.

"The good and bad about one company controlling these numbers is that while you don't have to shop around for competitive prices, you are gonna be locked in to whatever they charge. I'd check out Bowker's website to see what they're charging currently. They offer steep discounts if you buy in bulk, plus the numbers don't expire, so you can buy and keep any number of ISBNs for the future.

"KDP and IngramSpark actually let you buy an ISBN from Bowker through their website at a discounted rate. This saves you some money and adds a lot of convenience, but you don't get the bulk discounts Bowker offers. If you're going to buy multiple ISBNs, you probably want to go directly through Bowker.

"Oh, by the way, The fascinating thing about–"

Before Richard can finish his sentence, you hear a loud pop, like a small firecracker, and an angry shout from Grandalf. A second later, Buttercup scampers onto the left side of the screen, cackling maniacally.

"RUN AWAY! Run away, Richard!"

Richard eyes the corner of the screen, where some kind of digital haze is starting to leak out–smoke, maybe? He cautiously edges off to the other side, and Buttercup turns to look at you, beaming.

"My turn! What's next?"

"Could you show me how to submit my book for printing?"

<Turn to page 43>

"I know what's needed for printing, but what about audio recording? How do I set up my space?"

<Turn to page 48>

"I'm ready to record! How do I make my voice sound amazing?"

<Turn to page 62>

WHAT'S THE PROCESS FOR GETTING MY BOOK PRINTED?

Digital smoke pours out from the left corner of your screen. Richard ducks off to the right, peaking out pensively. Buttercup strides to the center of your screen, talking at you as if nothing odd is happening.

"So, you ready to take on the dreadful dumpster fire of a path to get your book printed yourself?"

Richard gives an audible groan and pinches the bridge of his nose as he finally disappears offscreen.

Buttercup cups their hand to their face and whispers surreptitiously, "Okay, so it's not actually that bad of a process. But if you haven't done it before, it is A LOT of steps to learn."

You consider looking for a pen and paper to start writing things down, but Buttercup scoffs at you and points to the top corner of the screen, where a blank document opens and a number 1 appears.

Buttercup hops to the side and as they speak, words begin typing themselves out.

"One: The **front cover** must be designed to the specs of the printer, accounting for page count, spine size, cover material (hardcover or paperback), and image ppi (that's pixels per inch).

"Two: The **back cover** is also included in this, and it must have the ISBN number plus barcode along with whatever content you want on the back.

"Three: If you want a **dust jacket**, you'll need those measurements, fold lines, and the written content for the inside folds.

"Four: You'll need to choose the order and content of your **front matter**: title page, copyright page, dedication, table of contents, author's note, et cetera. Similarly, you'll need to sort out your **back matter**: epilogue, glossary, acknowledgements, afterword, and so on.

"Five: For the **main text**, you are expected to have a consistent chapter heading design, page numbers on opposing sides (even on the left, odd on the right), author name in the header or footer on one side, book title on the other, and no page numbers or headers/footers on pages with chapter headings.

"Six: **Text** should typically be a consistent font, be sized between 10 and 12 points, have consistent line spacing throughout, and have paragraphs automatically indented (no manually tabbed paragraphs!).

"Seven: **Images** should be consistent in size and positioning throughout, and they should meet the ppi and resolution requirements of the printer.

"Eight: You need to choose a **paper quality** (color, weight, edging), **ink** (color, grayscale, black and white), and a **finish** (glossy or matte).

"Nine: Lastly, the trickiest part: **the margins**. After choosing your book size, you need to choose the margins that will go on the top, bottom, and outside page edges (these don't have to match). Then you need to calculate the gutter margin (that's the inner edge of the pages)—this will depend on how thick your book is. The more pages your book has, the deeper your pages will bend at the center, which means the bigger the gutter margin needs to be to make up for that lost space."

You blink several times, eyes now dry from reading along. Buttercup nods knowingly and waves a hand, the document saving to your desktop.

"Now, if you are willing to pay an illustrator a little bit, you can find someone who has created book covers for publishers, so they will already know the requirements to meet, which will save you a lot of tedium."

Buttercup starts to nod, mumbling to themself, then stops and holds up a hand. "Wait—one more thing! Along with the design of the book, you will need to provide some metadata. Richard?"

Covering his mouth and nose with a handkerchief, Richard makes his way on screen, standing very close to the right-hand edge. "Online sellers will ask you for keywords, audience ages, and genre categories, so be sure to have those ready! They're a great, free opportunity for SEO—search engine optimization, if you don't know—and marketing, so you don't want to be making them up on the fly last minute."

Buttercup looks back at you expectantly before asking, "Ok, what next?"

"A place to record?"

<Turn to page 48>

"I have a recording room set up, but what tech do I need?"

<Turn to page 54>

"I really don't want to record my own audio. How do I hire a narrator?"

<Turn to page 76>

A PLACE TO CALL RECORDING HOME?

You look over at Richard, but he shakes his head. “Oh, I’m not teaching you about sound. They are,” he says, pointing over at Buttercup in the corner of the screen. “I’m just here to keep things on track.”

Grandalf seems to have disappeared, but you hear a distant, disembodied voice say with a chuckle, “A bard is always late.”

Buttercup sticks out their tongue at that, then they look at you with an excited . . . well, menacing gleam in their eyes. “You said you were ready, so let’s get started! The biggest thing you need to focus on is putting together a room you can record in that is both soundproofed and sound treated.

"People often say these as if they are interchangeable, but the truth is that they serve totally different purposes. Soundproofing is how you keep sound from getting inside the room, whereas sound treatment is how you make the sound nice to listen to. Since the first thing we need to do is stop the sound, let's start with soundproofing.

"The general idea is this: the more shit you put in the way of the sound, the quieter the inside will be. Think of it like weatherproofing a house. You want to close the windows and doors, seal all the entrances up with weather stripping, and add as much dense insulation fluff as you can. Density is your friend. Think air-tight room."

They giggle a bit too gleefully before finishing, "BUT! Don't forget to leave yourself some pathways for oxygen."

"Now, as to where to put it, you're generally best off if you can get it to the middle of your home, but in cases where you live in a noisy area, put it on the side of the home farthest away from the noisiest place. Roads, bars, clubs—all of these produce noise, so get as far as you can from them. And for god's sake, turn off the AC and washing machines!"

You hear Richard give a little snort.

"You'll have the easiest time if you put your recording space into a small room, like a closet, but the danger is that you might end up sounding like you're trapped in a cardboard box if it's too small. If you have one, a walk-in closet would work best. Or a bedroom. Just remember that as the room gets bigger, you'll need more sound treatment."

Buttercup stops and looks at you to gauge where you're at. Clearly liking what they see, they continue, "Good. You seem quick, so I'm going to move on to the sound treatment side. May as well oil while the gears are turning!

"For sound treatment, you're dealing with three general ranges: bass frequencies, mid frequencies, and high frequencies." They pause while ticking off their fingers, then say, "Just switch out the word 'sound' for 'frequencies' and you're there.

"Anyway, for all of these frequencies, your best bet is to make or get absorption panels to deal with the sound. If the absorption panel is around 4 inches thick, it will deal with the low stuff. If the absorption panel is in the 1.5 to 2 inch range, it will hit the mids and the highs.

"They're not super hard or expensive to build—YouTube university can get you what you need. The key thing is to hang them around the room until you stop hearing echoes and deep, boomy sounds. You want to hear just your own voice, with no trace of the room you're recording in.

"If you've hung panels all around the room and you're still hearing things, try hanging one or two horizontally from the ceiling. This is called an acoustic cloud, and they can sometimes help in rooms that are finicky."

They take a deep breath and look at you with amber eyes that are both too big and too murdery to stare back at comfortably. "This whole process is really more of a guess-and-check type game unless you understand the physics of it, so move things around until you're happy with how it sounds.

"The last thing I'll say with this is make sure that your computer is either solid state–read 'silent'–or *outside* your recording room. So many people spend a month making the perfect room only to ruin it by putting their computer fan just a few feet from their mic. Don't trip the finish line."

As you nod your head, Richard taps a glittering wristwatch, coughing pointedly. Buttercup says, "Yes, yes, I get it, no need to be such a di–Richard.

"Okay, sounds like you're ready to get into the technicalities of recording! Or would you like to jump forward?"

"Now that I've got a room, what tech do I need?"

<Turn to page 54>

"How do I actually record my voice?"

<Turn to page 62>

"I don't know if I can get my space where it needs to be. How do I hire a narrator?"

<Turn to page 76>

WHAT TECH DO I NEED?

You close your eyes for a second to let everything sink in. When you open them again, the screen has gone an ominous shade of blue, and some garbled text and wingdings fill the screen.

Maybe your computer really *does* need a reboot. As you reach for the power button, the screen suddenly flickers, and you hear what sounds like the old internet dial up sound . . . but blown through a war horn? Your normal computer screen appears, save for a few blue pixels.

Grandalf walks on screen and waves his hand, brushing away the pixels like annoying bits of dust.

"Well now, it appears things got a little overheated with all that back and forth. I do apologize. But I come back to you now at the turn of the screen.

"So where were we? Tech? Oh dear . . . That's not exactly an area I'm knowledgeable in . . ." Grandalf mumbles a bit, then pulls out a little brown pipe and starts puffing on it. As he concentrates, pixelated little clouds of smoke swirl up over his head.

"Well, let's try and make the best of it. Now, assuming you've got a nice, treated space that doesn't have a bunch of nasty noises, you need to invest in some gear. This is where a budget can be most useful. If you want a setup that lifts you up to the highest peak of expertise, you're looking at about $1,000 worth of gear. If you want a more basic setup, the lowest reasonable cost should be around $300."

Grandalf suddenly lifts up his staff and taps it in front of him, audibly knocking on the glass of the monitor screen. "But *never* forget the best money saver when looking for quality tech: buy used. You can get an expert-level setup for $500 to $600. Got it?" He stares at you until you nod.

"Hmph, good. Now, since you obviously have a computer already, here are the other items you need: a mic, a mic cable, a mic stand, an audio interface, a pair of headphones, and a digital audio workstation."

You hear Buttercup's voice yell from offscreen, "It's called a *DAW*, old man."

"Ahem, right, right . . . And you'll need some new cables so you can hook up your computer outside the recording room. Probably several of those, what are they called . . . universal bus cables? Thumbdrive cables?"

Buttercup hops on screen with a pronounced eyeroll. "U-S-B cables. I think it's time for me to take over now," they say as they cross their arms.

"Yes, yes, quite right. I'll think I'll just pop out for a pint . . ." he says and eagerly scoots off.

"Ok, great!" Buttercup says, interlacing their fingers and cracking their knuckles. "Let's talk mics. You're gonna want to get either a shotgun or a condenser microphone with an XLR cable. These generally have the best sound quality, but make sure you get one that has a low noise floor. That just means the company worked hard to make sure all the circuitry doesn't fuck up the sound. I wouldn't spend less than $100 on a mic, as the materials companies use get *really* cheap below that.

"If the mic doesn't come with one already, get an XLR cable–the cylindrical fat one with 3 prongs inside. It's what connects the mic to the audio interface, and it's normally shielded to make sure that your system doesn't pick up any of the electronic hum your devices put out. *Shielded* is your friend. *Unshielded* is basically an enormous radio antenna.

"Mics sometimes come with their own stands, but if you want one that isn't crappy, shop around for either a boom arm you can attach to the wall or desk, or one of those mic stands your high school chorus used to use."

They pause to take a deep breath before launching into a quick stream of sentences. "For the audio interface, you're gonna want to go with one of the known brands, like Focusrite, M-Audio, Behringer, or Universal Audio. There's a lot of complicated circuitry that goes into making a good interface, and if you use a cheap brand, you're gonna pay for it with crappy sound. You'll likely have a crackling or hissing sound in your recording that you won't know how to get rid of, and it'll ruin an otherwise great recording."

They clap as they get more animated and start pacing back and forth across the screen. "It's well and good putting the sound into your computer, but you also need to be able to listen to what you're doing. Otherwise, you'll get to the end of the recording and find out that you made a bunch of mistakes and random noises. In order to minimize that, you'll need a good pair of cans."

They stop their pacing to stare at you pointedly, making sure you get the innuendo. With a cackle, they continue, "Cans are another name for headphones. Get a good quality pair, somewhere in the $50 to $100 range, and keep an eye out for the keyword 'Studio Monitor.' A lot of headphones try to make your listening experience 'prettier' by using effects that alter the sound input, but you don't want that. You want ones that are honest and . . . flat." They smirk at you, then resume pacing.

"Lastly, you're going to want to get familiar with a DAW of your choice. This is the program you'll use to record your voice. There are free ones like Audacity, but these lack a lot of features and are what is called a 'destructive recording environment.' Basically, each time you edit the audio, you make a permanent change to the sound, which is locked in once you save the recording. So no going back.

"There are a ton of paid ones, but the highlights to know are Logic Pro, Adobe Audition, Reaper, and Twisted Wave. These are all non-destructive, so you can apply effects to the sound without permanently altering the recording."

They finally stop, and you both take a big breath. Buttercup smiles at you happily. "I know that was a lot, but that pretty much covers the tech side of things. We can launch into recording, if you're ready. What do you say?"

You see Richard peak his head in hopefully as your next three choices appear on the screen.

"I'm ready. How do I record my voice?"

<Turn to page 62>

"How do I edit the audio and turn it into a finished book?"

<Turn to page 68>

"This is getting complicated and expensive. How do I go about hiring a narrator?"

<Turn to page 76>

How do I record my voice?

Richard heaves a dramatic sigh and disappears. Buttercup looks at you happily, unphased. "Ah, my favorite part! There's nothing like leaping into a character's mind and playing around inside."

Seeing concern rise on your face, they add quickly, "Acting! Not messing around with their brain. Though that can be fun too." They giggle gleefully.

Richard calls from offscreen, "Buttercup, you promised to stay focused."

"Can't have any fun around you two wrinklies," they grumble. "To get started, you're going to want to open up your DAW and make sure that all the tech is connected correctly.

"It should go mic to audio interface via XLR cable, with a USB cable connecting the audio interface to the computer. Get as long of a cable as you need to keep the computer outside of the room.

"Once you do that, make sure that the DAW is using your audio interface as the input device. You *definitely* don't want to use your computer mic for this. It'll be really far away and sound like absolute shit." They cup their hands around their mouth to muffle the sound and echo the last word repeatedly.

"Next, make sure you have a track armed for recording. You can do a few tests to make sure, but when you hit record, you should see the track move, and something called a waveform will start to form in response to your voice. It's basically a wiggly line or shadow that represents the sounds you're making." As they say this, Buttercup dances around a bit, gesturing the wiggles with their arms.

"When you actually start recording, you're going to make mistakes. That's normal when learning any new skill. I've been recording for more than 5 years, and I still make mistakes all the time. The important thing is figuring out a good system for marking the mistakes or recording over them.

"There's a technique we use called 'click recording' that is the easiest way to mark a mistake, in my oh-so-*humble* opinion," they say, giving a mocking bow. "Each time you make a mistake in the recording, either use something like a dog clicker or snap your fingers to make a sharp noise. You'll see it later as a vertical spike in the recording and will be able to see each place you made a mistake. That way, when you go back to edit the track, it'll be easy to skip to those specific spots instead of having to listen through the entire thing."

They pause to draw a wiggly red line across the screen with one big spike in the middle.

"At the end of the day, 'punch and roll' is gonna be the best system for cleaning up the mistakes. Each time you make a mistake, go back 10 seconds on the original track and record over it." They walk over to the spike in the line, then walk back a few steps and mark an X. "So you start here, picking up with whatever word or line starts here, then record over the mistake and roll seamlessly into the section past it." They wipe out the spike in the line then mark another X a few steps after it.

"Jumping in can take some getting used to, but if you can program some hotkeys to help jump around the track, it goes really fast." They make a dramatic flourish at the red spike, and it blinks a few times onscreen, then disappears. "From there, it's just a matter of hitting record and working your way through the book. Just keep paying attention to marking those mistakes as you go, because going back through a multiple-hour recording to find them is a bitch and a half.

"If you need to estimate how long it will take you to record the book, assume you'll take about 6 to 10 working hours for every 10,000 words. You'll definitely get faster as you go, but as a new narrator, the worst thing you can do is assume you'll be fast. If you quote a publisher or your audience a really quick timeline, you may end up exceptionally stressed and burn out your voice, and then it's gonna take a *really* long time. No one's gonna be mad if you get it done quicker than your estimate."

Buttercup takes a deep breath, tapping their chin contemplatively. "Yup, I think that's all I have for—" Richard bounds on screen suddenly, cutting them off.

"Are we moving on from tech? Can we talk business now?" he asks.

They both turn to look at you. "What do you want to learn next?"

"How do I go about editing the audio?"

<Turn to page 68>

"This is way more than I bargained for. How do I hire a narrator?"

<Turn to page 76>

How do I go about editing the audio?

Buttercup turns and blows a big raspberry at Richard. "Not your turn yet!" Richard pouts and pops off screen again, mumbling something about "tech nerds."

Looking very pleased with themself, Buttercup turns and interlaces their fingers in front of them in a sagely manner. "Editing and mastering is a long process, but a rewarding one. Downside is you'll have to listen to your voice for hours on end. Upside is you now get to make a ton of creative choices that can add to the finished audiobook in amazing ways.

"The first thing you need to do is edit out all the mistakes. If you marked your mistakes with a click, you should be able to see a bunch of lines on your recording that show you where they are. Go to each click and cut the recording so that you can delete the mistake and move the sound around. If you did punch and roll, you can skip this step entirely!

"After that, it's time to move the dialogue around and modify the breaths between sentences. Whenever people are talking to each other, you want it to sound real and alive. In real life, people tend to talk right on top of each other, sometimes even interrupting each other, so your recording should reflect that. Just make sure that it doesn't sound too cramped. Sometimes silence is just as important as constant talking.

"Now, depending on your story, you may have characters talking from other places—say, over the phone or radio. Alternatively, someone may need a big, booming voice, like a god speaking from on high. In these moments, you can add effects to the track that will make them sound like you want them to. This can be tricky, but I think it's worth it. It usually involves adding equalization, distortion, reverb, or some combination of the three.

They point at three spots above their head and the words "Equalization," "Distortion," and "Reverb" appear on the screen.

"Equalization, or EQ, basically lets you change the sound in specific frequencies. You can raise, lower, or cut them out completely. This is super useful when you wanna make a voice sound more electronic. Since most speakers or phones cut out all the high and low sounds of a recording, you can use EQ to get the right robotic or techno vibe.

"Distortion adds a bunch of extra noise to the sound, like how a metal band has that gravelly, grungy sound. You can say it makes the sound *crunchy.* This is good for people talking on a radio or satellite phone.

"Reverb copies what happens in an actual room. When a sound is made in an untreated room, it makes all the surfaces vibrate and send that sound back to you. It's kind of like an echo, but it's a bunch of tiny echoes all adding together to make the reverb. Used right, this is a great way to do THE GOD EFFECT," Buttercup finishes.

They wave a hand and the words disappear. "ARE YOU READY FOR . . . mastering?" they ask with a big grin, continuing in their affected, announcer-y voice.

You nod and they give a small skip. "Then let's get to it! Mastering is the process of finishing the audio so that all the different tracks come together to give a full sound without overwhelming each other.

"For audiobooks, this is usually relatively simple, as you don't often have more than one track making sound at any given time. But there are still some things you need to make sure you do. Generally speaking, those should be . . ." Here they start ticking off fingers. "Noise removal, equalization, compression, make-up gain, and limiting.

"Noise removal is a process where you can tell the program what sounds in your space are unwanted. To do this, record 10 seconds of your room with no other sounds. No breathing, no shuffling, no speaking. Then put these 10 seconds into a noise subtractor and apply that subtractor to the track.

"For equalization, you want to cut out all frequencies below 50 Hz. This should cut out engines and machine noise. You also want to cut out all frequencies above 10,000 Hz, as this is mostly just electronic hiss. Everything else should largely be handled by your sound treatment and mic technique, but definitely test things to get the best sound. Less is more.

"Compression is how you get all the loud parts of your recording a little closer to the quiet parts. You don't want to go too hard here–keep it less than 4 decibels of reduction at a time. If you need to reduce the volume more than that, run a second compressor.

"Once you've reduced the loudness with compression, you're going to need to bump the sound back up. You can do this with make-up gain. Make-up gain will normally be part of your compressor. Again, keep this below 4 decibels of change. That way it's not too aggressive.

"The last step is making sure you're not losing audio. When the sound gets too loud, you get something called clipping. This is when the system gets overwhelmed and you lose sound quality. You know, like when a streamer loses their shit and starts screaming into the mic." They get a fond, faraway look in their eyes. "That weird cut you hear in the sound is them clipping.

"A limiter compresses any sound over the volume you set down to exactly that volume. For audiobooks, you want your limiter set to negative 3 decibels. This is the maximum that most audiobook distributors allow in their systems."

They stop and stare at you meaningfully for a moment. "This is the place you're most likely to get hung up. Audiobook platforms are incredibly strict with their requirements, so you may have to mess around with your settings until you meet the requirements.

"If your audio is too loud, consider reducing the make-up gain and applying more compression. If too quiet, do the opposite. If your 'noise floor is too high,' try applying noise reduction or using a noise gate. Noise gates should be a last resort though, 'cause they make the audio sound really strange. Our ears aren't used to rooms being completely silent, so it makes the audio feel . . . not normal.

"Key takeaway: figure out a chain of effects that works well for your room and your platforms and stick to it like glue. It'll take practice, but with time you can make it work.

"And that's about all I've got for the audio side!" They take a deep bow. "Richard, would you like to come out now?"

As Richard strides on screen, the following options appear above the two characters:

"I really don't want to do all this work. How do I hire a narrator?"

<Turn to page 76>

"Once I'm done, how do I upload my work to a distribution platform?"

<Turn to page 82>

How do I hire a narrator?

"*Finally*, it's my turn!" Richard says, then thumps Buttercup on the back with a double-clicking sound. "Thanks, toots. I got it from here."

"*Toots*? Ugh." Buttercup shudders a little, then takes a little jump and disappears below the edge of the screen. "I'll be here when you need me!"

Richard adjusts his tie and straightens his suit jacket before beginning. "Hiring a narrator is pretty straightforward. You need to pick a demo section from your book, find someone within your budget, and get them under contract.

"First step is to pick a portion of your book that you like. It should have both high and low energies, be exciting to read, and have a few different characters speaking. That will give you the opportunity to hear how the narrator will voice your characters and help you get a sense for the quality of their acting.

"Next, you need to figure out what style of narration you want. Narration can be done one of four ways: solo, dual, duet, and full cast.

"Solo is the cheapest and most common. It's one narrator, narrating every character, across the whole book.

"Dual is next, where you have one masculine voice and one feminine one, and they split the chapters based on whether the primary character is masc or femme. That means they'll be voicing all the characters and all the narration within one chapter. This is pretty common in stories with multiple POVs.

"Duet is going to be more complicated—and thus more expensive—than the other two, as it requires a lot more engineering and collaboration. Regardless of the perspective, the two narrators will split all the dialogue according to the character speaking. As for the narration sections, you'll need to discuss who you want for that with your narrators.

"Finally, full cast narration is going to be the most expensive option. Each character across the whole story will be voiced by a separate actor. These are most common with a celebrity cast for a high profile book, but there are many producers who would be willing to help you put together a full cast version for a fee. Are you with me?"

As you nod, Richard continues, "So after you've got a sample and you've got a style, you need to find a narrator. Narrators on places like Fiverr and Upwork are cheaper, but they're going to be less flexible.

"Narrators with their own businesses are going to be more willing to negotiate. They might be able to give you discounts for volume, connect you with other narrators for different narration styles, or even set up contracts that allow you to lower the initial cost for yourself.

"The third option is going through ACX, Amazon's Audible Creation Exchange–the place where Audible sources most of its books. The narrators there are freelance and often on the cheaper end. However, if you do something like Royalty Share or Royalty Share Plus, just keep in mind that you'll be required to keep all sales through Amazon, and Amazon's royalties are *high*. At maximum, you're getting 40%, and that's if you don't split those royalties with the narrator.

"Bottom line: figure out a narration budget that works for you, then pursue a narrator who can work with you on that. And remember that people running their own businesses can negotiate and be flexible on royalty agreements, or at least less restrictive than corporations.

"Once you've found a narrator or a few narrators you like, agreed on a price, and agreed on a deadline, you'll need to agree on milestones. Often narrators will have an early check-in to make sure the style is right, then one or two more at the halfway point and the end. This way you can make sure they're sticking to the overall vision and haven't wandered off the tracks with voices, accents, or emotional inflection. That being said, if they don't want to agree on check-ins at all, this is a pretty major red flag.

"Once you've agreed on everything, hand over the full manuscript and wait for the magic. These artists can do some incredible stuff, often bringing things to life in a way you never imagined. There'll probably be a bit of back and forth to make sure that everyone is on the same page in the beginning, but once they get going, you should be good.

"The finished product should consist of opening credits that say who wrote the book and who narrated it, each audio chapter, closing credits, and a retail audio sample.

"The retail audio sample is a selection of audio from the book that people can listen to when they're browsing your distributor's platform. You want it to be quick and punchy, getting listeners excited for your book."

Richard clasps his hands together in excitement and says, "And now all that's left is the wrap!"

Buttercup clambers up from below the screen, looking as if they just tunneled out of the ground. "Oh, is it time for the distribution phase?"

"Yeah. How do I upload all this to the distributors?"

<Turn to the next page.>

How do I upload to the distribution platforms?

Richard walks over to one side of the screen and says, "I think we could all contribute to this one. Grandalf, care to join us?"

There is a small, sparkly poof and Grandalf appears between the two, twirling his staff. "Ah, so is the real journey about to begin? Excellent news."

"Fire away, tiny," Richard says, ceding the center of the screen to Buttercup.

"Why thanks, big Dick! Whether you recorded things yourself or hired out, you should have all your audio files ready. Opening credits, chapters, closing credits, and retail audio sample. Take these files to the distribution platform and start uploading!

"Depending on the platform, you may need to claim your book title if you've already published the printed version. For example, if you go to ACX, you'll need to let them know your account is linked to KDP. Then you can tell the site what books are yours. If you don't see them, you should be able to use the search bar to find 'em. Make sure the original text has been approved, or it won't show up on the marketplace.

"Once you've picked your book, you can go to the audio upload section and start putting in your files. Most platforms use a simple drag and drop method, so putting them in should be pretty easy.

Grandalf mentions from the back, "Though if you aren't orderly with your file naming, things could get more complicated!

Richard steps up and says, "If any of your files don't pass inspection, you may need to go back and edit them or talk to your narrator about getting them fixed. Good narrators should use some verification processes to make sure that their audio will pass inspection, but just in case they don't, you need to keep in contact with them so that they can help you fix any issues.

"After all that, your book should just need to go through internal verification. Usually that's someone listening to the book on the corporate side and checking to make sure that nothing sounds wrong or was credited incorrectly.

Grandalf jumps in to say, "And once all that checks out, you will become the proud owner of a brand new audiobook!"

Buttercup looks at the two of them and then at you. "I'm gonna miss this. The folks I work with aren't nearly as quick learners as you are."

Grandalf puts his hand on their shoulder and says, "Come now, Buttercup, you knew this was going to be over eventually."

"Yeah, I was just hoping they'd be dumber so I could keep teaching them stuff."

Richard laughs. “Yeah, it is a real shame they’re not a total dumbass.”

“You know that’s not what I meant,” Buttercup says with a glower.

Richard pats their back and says, “We know, Dandy.”

Grandalf looks out at you through the screen. “It has truly been a pleasure sharing what we know. But, here at last, dear friend, is the end of our fellowship in these electronic pages. Go with your newfound knowledge.”

He reaches out to put both arms around the other two, who look a bit dejected. Smiling as kindly as pixels can emote, Grandalf says, “I will not ask you not to weep, any of you. For not all tears are evil. This is merely goodbye, not the end.”

With that, the three disappear from your screen with a pop, leaving you where you started, staring at the blinking cursor at the end of a finished book.

Quest Complete

CHEAT SHEET

Step 1: Beta readers.

Step 2: Editing. There are 3 types:

Developmental. This covers a deep analysis of the plot, story structure, and characters, aiming to improve the overall narrative to make the story shine.

Copyediting. Sometimes called line editing, this involves cleaning up the story by correcting grammar, continuity errors, and weak syntax.

Proofreading. Usually done right before printing, this final step targets minor mistakes, typos, and any book formatting errors.

Step 3: Book formatting. This involves deciding how the book will look visually. This can be broken down into the following:

Book size. Base your choice in size on the common sizing for your book's genre.

Margins. These can be different on each side of the page, but they should be wide enough to give the text some breathing room and not make the reader feel claustrophobic. Check the recommended gutter size according to how many pages are in your book.

Font choice. Different fonts convey different emotions and produce different reading experiences. Stick to popular, easy-to-read fonts for the main text. Keep things simplistic and consistent to give a professional feel.

Chapter headings. These headings can be minimal or have an artistic flourish; choose a font, text size, positioning, and if there will be any accompanying illustrations.

Widows and orphans. Avoid having a single word or line on one full page. Research standard formatting "tricks" to avoid these or rewrite some sentences.

Programs. There are many options to choose from that could fit your needs: Adobe InDesign (monthly fee, advanced program, industry standard), Scrivener (flat cost, all-in-one program, complex), Atticus (high cost, all-in-one program, streamlined), and Microsoft Word (affordable, basic, limited formatting capabilities).

Front matter. This can include the title page, copyright page, and personal notes, like a dedication or an author's note.

Back matter. This can include things like an epilogue, glossary, acknowledgments, and afterword.

Main text. Internal illustrations should be consistent in size, positioning, ppi, and resolution. Know standard formatting rules for page number positioning.

Overall, formatting should feel invisible; poor formatting is distracting at minimum and actively off-putting at worst.

Step 4: Book cover illustration. You can use Adobe Illustrator, Photoshop, Canva, or a platform that generates standardized book covers. If you hire an illustrator, you can hire artists from places like Instagram, Fiverr, or other similar platforms. Remember to ask about the use of AI if that matters to you.

Step 5: Get an ISBN. To own the ISBN yourself, you will need to buy them from Bowker if you live in the US. Bowker offers steep discounts if you buy a bundle.

- You need a different ISBN for each version of your book: paperback, hardback, and audiobook.
- ISBNs are not required for eBooks, though distributors like bookshops often expect them.
- KDP and IngramSpark offer free ISBNs through their service, but these are owned by them and will restrict your book sales to their platforms.

These platforms also offer an option to buy ISBNs from Bowker at a discounted rate. You will own this ISBN, but you do not get the bundled discount Bowker offers if you want to buy multiple.

Step 6: Print the book. Know your page count, cover type, and ISBN. You'll need to choose paper quality, ink color, and book cover finish.

Back cover should have a book blurb; it can also have an author blurb and/or reviews.

For hard covers, you can have a dust jacket with extra written content on the inside folds. Know your measurements and fold lines.

Distribution websites will ask you to provide keywords and one to three genre categories. Do some research on the best choices in order to improve SEO.

Step 7: Set up your audio recording room. There are two important processes for setting up a recording room:

- *Soundproofing.* This stops sound from getting inside the recording space. Dense materials do the most work here, so creating a room inside your house will give you the biggest leg up, followed by using an internal walk-in closet. Seal around doors and windows carefully, as sound will sneak in through any and all gaps.
- *Sound treatment.* This shapes the sound inside the room. Add bass traps and acoustic panels to remove echo, reverb, deep rumbles, and high, tinny sounds. Your voice should sound clean and natural, unaffected by the room.

Step 8: Get your audio tech: mic, XLR mic cable (shielded), mic stand, audio interface, headphones (studio monitor quality), and digital audio workstation (DAW).

Mics. Find a mic with a low noise-floor, neutral audio response, and pleasant sound. Look at offerings from Neumann, Rode, Audio-Technica, AKG, and Shure.

Mic stand. Look for a stand without springs because springs will vibrate when you talk. Make sure the stand is also compatible with your mic.

Headphones. The most important thing here is a neutral response. You want high quality, clean sound that hasn't been modified by the headphones themselves. Look for the tag "studio monitor."

Audio interface. A name brand is recommended here, as they are likely to have the cleanest pre-amps. Focusrite, M-Audio, Behringer, and Universal Audio all have solid offerings.

DAWs:

Adobe Audition: as an industry standard, Audition is a powerful tool with lots of fine control.

The subscription model could be a boon or bane, depending on your preferences.

Logic Pro: as another industry standard, Logic Pro is only available to Mac users, but it offers excellent functionality at a relatively high, one-time cost.

Reaper: less well known than Audition and Logic Pro, Reaper has most of the same functionality, but it requires some setup to get to know well. Metaphorically, if Adobe vs. Logic Pro are PC vs. Mac, Reaper is Linux.

Audacity: the biggest upside is the free cost; however, Audacity is a "destructive" recording environment, so any modifications you make to your voice are permanent and cannot be removed once you save and close the file.

Step 9: Record. Use a technique that allows you to mark your mistakes, like the click method or punch and roll. Make sure not to blow out your voice by recording too much at one time.

Step 10: Audio editing and mastering. Editing involves cutting together the audio files, clearing out mistakes, cleaning up breaths, and making the spaces between speeches natural to the ear. Mastering involves adding FX (audio effects) to the tracks to clean up the sound for distribution:

Equalization. Remove all frequencies below 50 Hz and above 10,000 Hz. Find and strengthen any frequencies that make your voice sound sweeter or more comfortable to the ear.

Compression. Lower the volume of the loudest sections of speech, but never more than 4 decibels at a time (use a second compressor if you need more). Add make-up gain to bring the volume of the whole track up so that it meets distributor specifications (not too loud, not too soft).

Limiting. Stop the volume of the audio from going above distributor requirement of -3 decibels.

Step 11: Upload the audiobook files!

About the Authors

Daniel Ryder is a voice actor and narrator with five years of experience in the industry. Their voice can be found in the Audible library, training materials for corporations like McDonald's and Hyundai, and a few (not particularly well-known) video games. They specialize in dynamic reads with casts of unique characters and love diving into the linguistic challenge of bringing believable accents to "real" characters. When they're not narrating, you can find them running a D&D campaign or getting lost in the middle of nowhere on their motorcycle.

Heather Ryder is an editor who has worked in all levels of the field for over ten years. When not editing a journal article or the latest in a series of fantasy novels, Heather can be found hiking, Pokémon Go-ing, reading, or some combination of the three. While she most often gravitates toward fiction, the technical work of editing scratches both sides of her brain pleasantly enough that she will happily work in almost any genre.

Thank you for reading our first instructional guidebook! If you like what we do and what we're about, please visit our website at www.inklingbookspublishing.com.

If you have questions for us or are interested in our services, please shoot us an email at daniel@inklingbookspublishing.com and/or heather@inklingbookspublishing.com.

www.ingramcontent.com/pod-product-compliance
Lightning Source LLC
Chambersburg PA
CBHW070640030426
42337CB00020B/4095

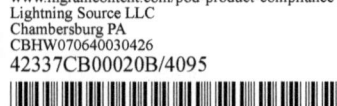

* 9 7 9 8 9 9 1 6 7 6 4 4 1 *